Texas
Grasslands

Includes:

Texas Ecoregions

Habitats and Habits

Bird Activities

Mammal Activities

Reptile & Amphibian Activities

Invertebrate Activities

Wildlife Respect

Waterford Press
www.waterfordpress.com

Introduction

Grasslands are defined as areas dominated by grasses, with tree or shrub canopies covering less than 25 percent of the area. In Texas, before European settlement, grasslands occupied about two-thirds of the landscape. In fact, more than 60% of Texas is grassland or prairie ecosystems. An ecosystem is a community of living organisms that interact with each other and their environment. Like Texans, grasslands are hardworking. The land, rivers, streams and lakes provide important habitats for many wild plants and animals and are very important to farmers and ranchers across the state.

Ecoregions are areas that share the same climate, geology, soils, wildlife and land formations. There are 10 different ecoregions in Texas.

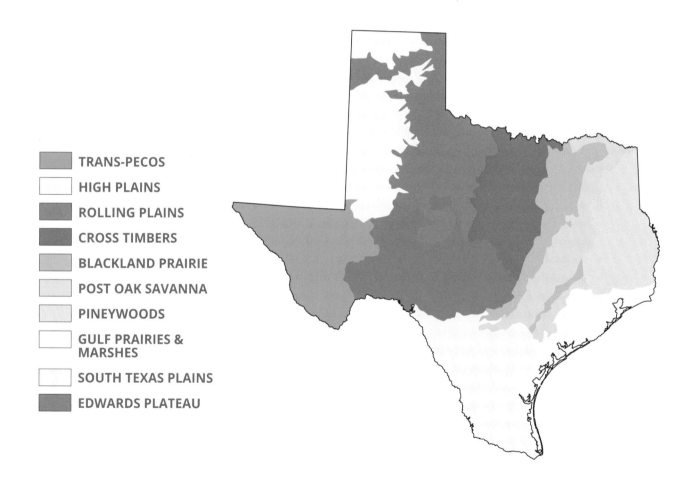

TRANS-PECOS

HIGH PLAINS

ROLLING PLAINS

CROSS TIMBERS

BLACKLAND PRAIRIE

POST OAK SAVANNA

PINEYWOODS

GULF PRAIRIES & MARSHES

SOUTH TEXAS PLAINS

EDWARDS PLATEAU

Texas Ecoregions

Trans-Pecos
From desert valleys and plains to wooded mountains,
the Trans-Pecos region extends from the far west
part of Texas to the Pecos River.

High Plains
The High Plains is a fairly level plateau. The
Caprock Escarpment separates it from the Rolling Plains.

Rolling Plains
The Rolling Plains is where many rivers and
tributaries in Texas begin.

Cross Timbers
The Cross Timbers area has a lot of trees as well as irregular prairies
and plains. It is found in north and central Texas.

Blackland Prairie
This region gets its name from the fertile,
black soils for which it is known.

Post Oak Savanna
There are many plants and animals here with ranges that extend as
far east as the forests and as far north as the Great Plains.

Pineywoods
The Pineywoods in East Texas are home to forests of tall hardwoods
and rolling hills covered with oaks and pines.

Gulf Prairies & Marshes
Streams and rivers divide this nearly level plain as
they flow into the Gulf of Mexico.

South Texas Plains
This region is known for its subtropical woodlands and
patches of palms, as well as thorny shrubs and trees.

Edwards Plateau
Known for spring-fed rivers and stony hills, Edwards Plateau is part of
an area sometimes called Texas Hill Country.

Class Act

Animals can be sorted into categories based on certain characteristics. The system for sorting animals into categories is called taxonomy. Mammals, birds, fish, reptiles and amphibians belong to a class of animals called vertebrates. Vertebrates are animals with backbones. Invertebrates are another class of animals that do not have backbones (like insects, worms, snails, lobsters, crabs and spiders).

Draw a line between the grassland animal and its class.

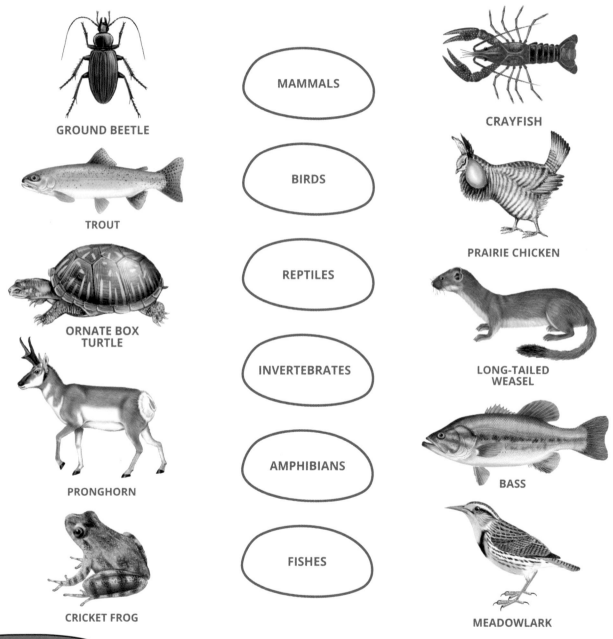

GROUND BEETLE

TROUT

ORNATE BOX TURTLE

PRONGHORN

CRICKET FROG

MAMMALS

BIRDS

REPTILES

INVERTEBRATES

AMPHIBIANS

FISHES

CRAYFISH

PRAIRIE CHICKEN

LONG-TAILED WEASEL

BASS

MEADOWLARK

You Are What You Eat

Herbivores eat mostly plants. Carnivores eat mostly animals.
Omnivores eat plants and animals.

Draw a line between the grassland animal and its diet.

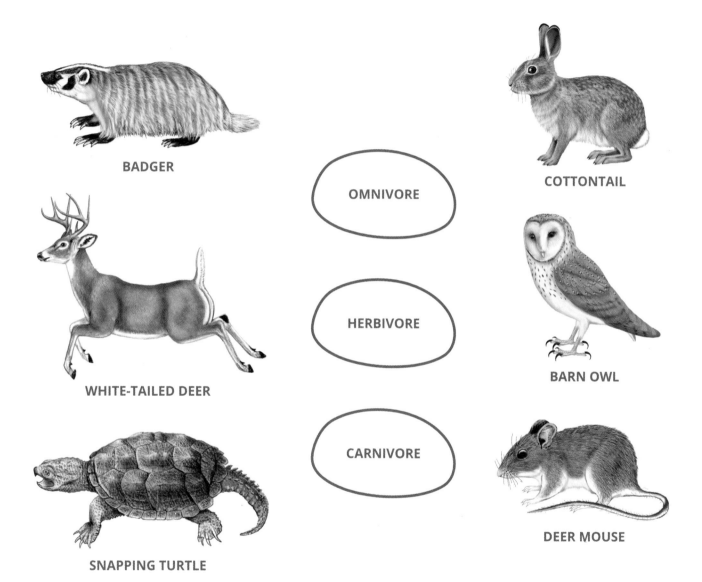

BADGER

OMNIVORE

COTTONTAIL

HERBIVORE

WHITE-TAILED DEER

BARN OWL

CARNIVORE

SNAPPING TURTLE

DEER MOUSE

Food Chain

A food chain is the order in which animals feed on other plants or animals.

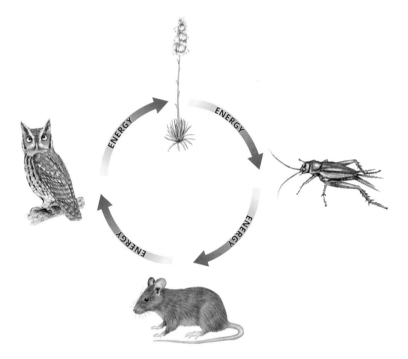

Producers – A producer takes the sun's energy and stores it as food.

Consumers – A consumer feeds on other living things to get energy. Consumers can include herbivores, carnivores and omnivores.

Decomposers – A decomposer consumes waste and dead organisms for energy.

Label each living organism below as a producer, consumer or decomposer.

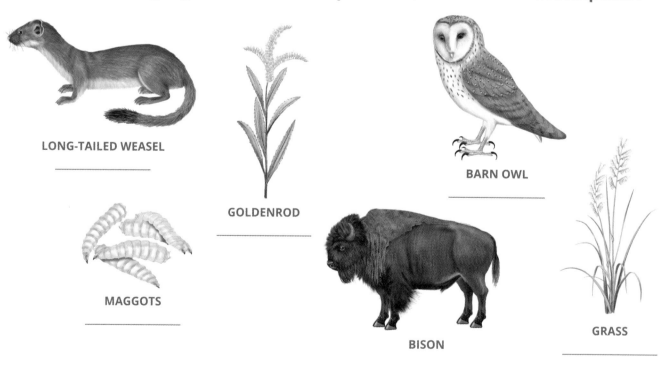

LONG-TAILED WEASEL

_____

GOLDENROD

_____

MAGGOTS

_____

BARN OWL

_____

BISON

_____

GRASS

_____

Find My Home

A habitat provides everything an animal needs for survival: food, shelter, water, the right temperature and protection from predators (animals who prey on other living things).

Draw a line between the animal and its habitat.

1.

BISON

2.

FROG

3.

HONEYBEE

4.

PRAIRIE DOG

(A)

A pond full of flies is where this hopping animal lives.

(B)

This buzzing animal lives in a honey-filled hive.

(C)

The wide open plains are where this big brown animal roams.

(D)

A hole in the ground makes a great home for this furry little creature.

Word Search

Birds that rely on grassland habitats for nesting are found across all 50 of the United States. Each grassland bird species has a unique set of habitat needs, but the Texas grasslands suit the needs of many.

Find the names of these important bird species in the puzzle.

SWALLOW

OWL

KILLDEER

BLUEBIRD

FALCON

SPARROW

WREN

PIPIT

LARK

Answers

```
L K A L K O L K A U W R R U L L K E
C P S L L I W A L L O O A A L P L A
F K R U L R L C R K U F O A P L S R
R E I C U E E L L K K W L S W A R T
L E B A C A L K D P W I O A T W P L
U L L E P S L N L E R R P A R F L F
P A W W U U D O W O E W I U P K N N
O O L R W W A C O L N R C A P L L S
E L E W E B R L P O P A N R O N P D
E C K R B S P A R R O W C P L I L L
S O W A L P F F P W O A P R I R I W
K F W N U N S S I E L L R A L P S C
R B T K E D N F I L L E L U R C I W
O L W L B E O R E R W N O A O W L T
A O W E I L L W R P S L A R E C U I
O P N L R W O L L A W S N S O O N N
B P L L D O S W A P A I S R B S O L
A R O N E S S B R R R S R A K P D K
```

Make Words

The **Eastern Meadowlark** is a beautiful, black and yellow grassland bird noted for its flute-like gurgling song.

How many words can you make from the letters in its name?

_____   _____

_____   _____

_____   _____

_____   _____

_____   _____

_____   _____

_____   _____

_____   _____

Answers

Possible answers include:
me, mew, mow, mad, maw, mar, ad, ark, ade, am, are, dam, doe, drew, deal, dark, dream, low, lad, led, lead, lark, mark, wear, red, row, read, real, meadow.

9

Spot The Differences

The **Greater Prairie Chicken** is a year-round resident of Texas and breeds from February to July. The male is known for his showy dance, boom and call as he tries to get female attention. This bird is an omnivore, feeding on insects, seeds, young grasses and other plants.

Can you spot five differences between the Greater Prairie Chicken pictures?

Answers

Word Search

As winter ends, the grasslands' small ponds and wetlands warm up first. These become homes to waterfowl and shorebirds who migrate from more southern latitudes, as well as stopovers for birds on their way north.

HERON

PELICAN

```
I N N A G L E D L E N O R O G T
O L H E A H R E R L T E E E E A
L O H L C I A A A P I A C H R N
L G N M R I O L N C C T I G E G
A L O O G T L E G R E T T P O G
G A T G R O H T E A P O O E N H
E A N T N O R E N N H O O S L N
L A E L C I A P R E E C P O O E
R E M S L G S I E O T I O O H O
A E N O A T G N T L N E E G R A
E E R M A N R E G T I P C E L O
P E L T R C I L A T N C L R M I
D C R E R G O I S P S O A O N I
R A R R M A L L A R D O N N G G
P L S T T I E E O P E E N A T E
T T R G T E N O C C E T L O D G
```

PINTAIL

COOT

EGRET

CRANE

MALLARD

GOOSE

Word Search

All North American mammals give birth to live young that feed on milk from their mother. Mammals are generally secretive in their habits and therefore difficult to spot in the field. Grasslands are some of the best places to look for them because they are often found seeking cover among scrub thickets and wood edges.

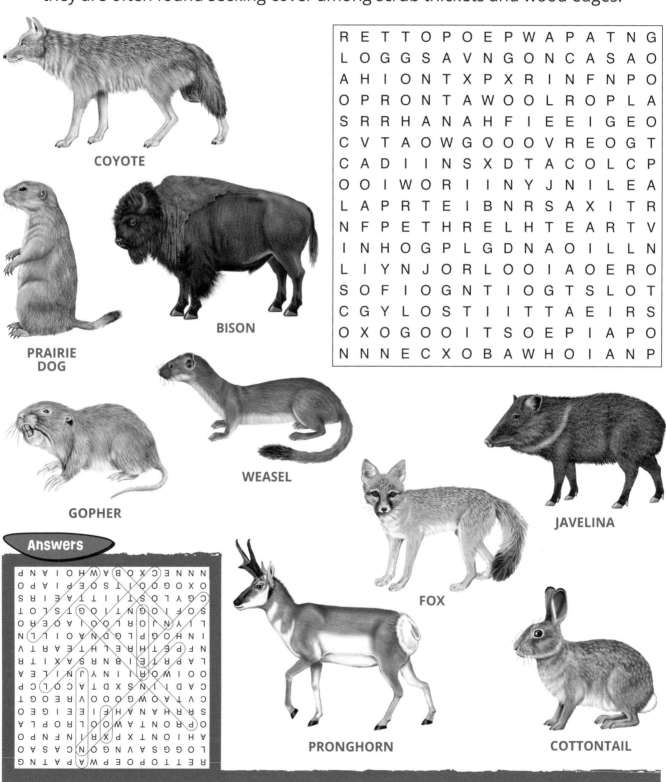

COYOTE

```
R E T T O P O E P W A P A T N G
L O G G S A V N G O N C A S A O
A H I O N T X P X R I N F N P O
O P R O N T A W O O L R O P L A
S R R H A N A H F I E E I G E O
C V T A O W G O O O V R E O G T
C A D I I N S X D T A C O L C P
O O I W O R I I N Y J N I L E A
L A P R T E I B N R S A X I T R
N F P E T H R E L H T E A R T V
I N H O G P L G D N A O I L L N
L I Y N J O R L O O I A O E R O
S O F I O G N T I O G T S L O T
C G Y L O S T I I T T A E I R S
O X O G O O I T S O E P I A P O
N N N E C X O B A W H O I A N P
```

PRAIRIE DOG

BISON

GOPHER

WEASEL

JAVELINA

FOX

PRONGHORN

COTTONTAIL

Answers

12

Origami

There are five species of wild cats found in Texas. Jaguar, Mountain Lion, Bobcat, Ocelot, and Jaguarundi are all either Texas natives now or have always been Texas natives.

Starting with a square piece of paper, follow the folding instructions to make this whimsical cat face.

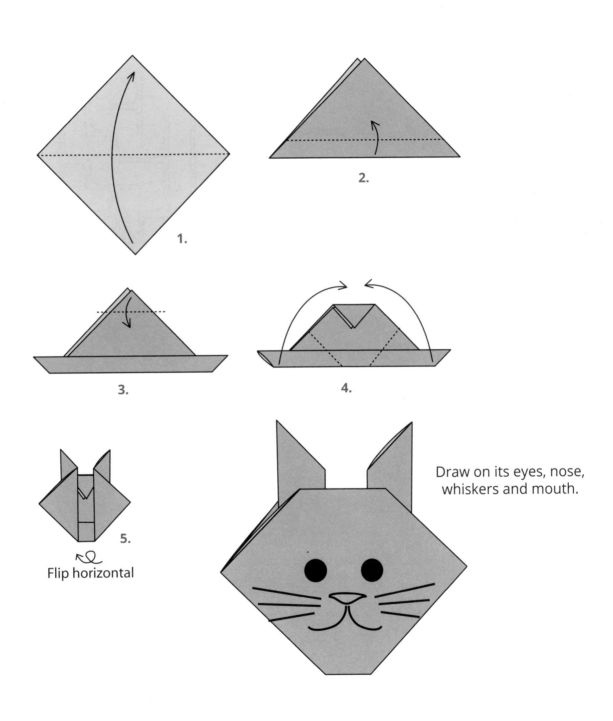

Draw on its eyes, nose, whiskers and mouth.

Maze

Help the Jackrabbit avoid its predators and find its burrow.

Color Me

In Texas, the **Pronghorn** is found only in the Trans-Pecos deserts and the High Plains. The only animal in the world with horns that branch, the pronghorn sheds them every year as though they were antlers.

Color this image to uncover its distinctive markings.

Color Key

Animal Tracks

Studying tracks is an easy way to discover the kinds of mammals found in an area.

Draw a line between the grassland mammal and its tracks.

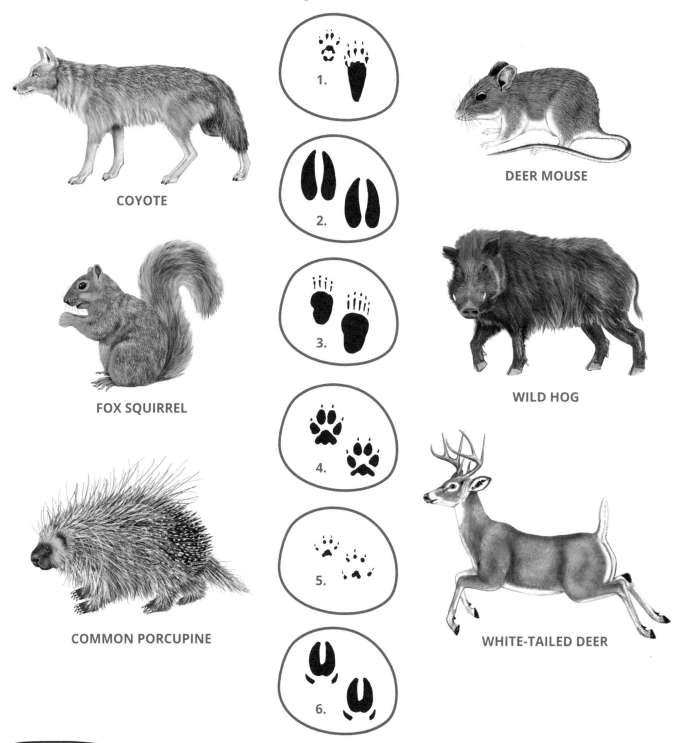

COYOTE

FOX SQUIRREL

COMMON PORCUPINE

1.

2.

3.

4.

5.

6.

DEER MOUSE

WILD HOG

WHITE-TAILED DEER

Make Words

The **Badger** is a fossorial animal. "Fossorial" means it is adapted to digging and lives mostly underground. It uses its long, front claws to dig in the ground to make a burrow and uses its back legs to kick out the dirt. It is known to dig faster than any mammal, including a man with a shovel. A badger usually dens in shallow burrows except during breeding season, when it will dig a nest chamber deep below the ground. The badger's black feet each have five toes, and the front feet have long, thick claws an inch or more in length. It has small eyes and ears and a slightly pointed nose. Its keen sense of smell is second only to that of members of the dog family.

How many words can you make from the letters in its name?

_____   _____

_____   _____

_____   _____

_____   _____

_____   _____

_____   _____

Origami

The **Deer Mouse** is one of North America's most abundant mammals. Its one-ounce body has a long, thin tail, and it is well-suited to a variety of habitats. This mouse's range extends from far northern Canada to Mexico and from the west to east coasts, except for some parts of the southeast.

Starting with a square piece of paper, follow the folding instructions below to create a mouse.

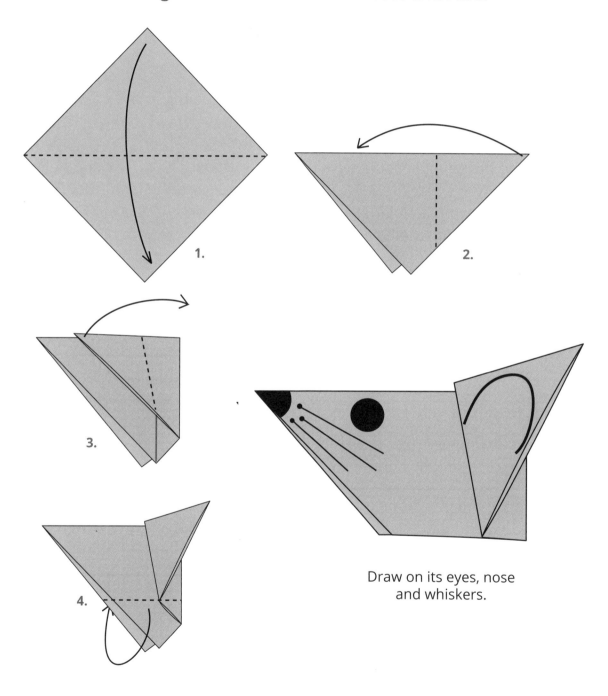

Draw on its eyes, nose and whiskers.

Be An Artist

The largest land animal in North America, the **American Bison** is one of the most well-known symbols of the American west. Once almost extinct, herds are now present in many states and number in the tens of thousands. The Official Texas State Bison Herd at Caprock Canyon State Park is the only remaining herd of the unique Southern Plains variety.

Draw this bison by copying one square at a time.

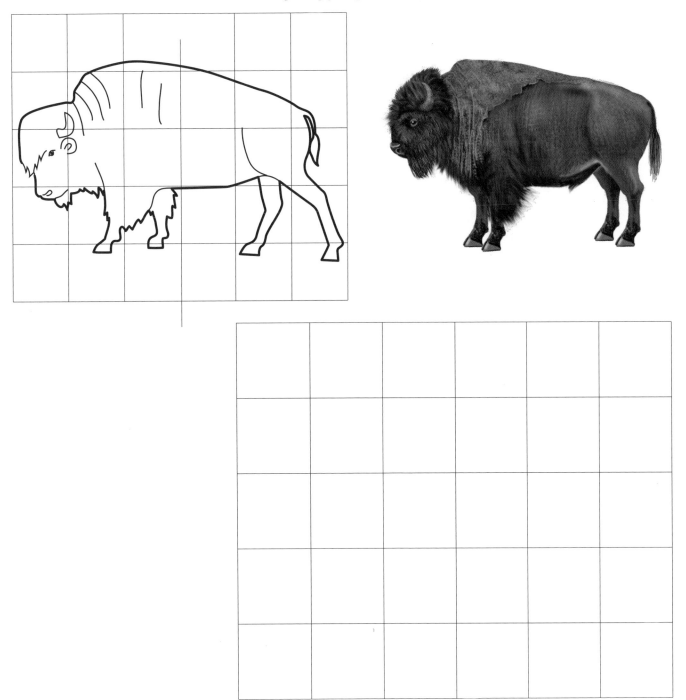

Maze

The **Black-tailed Prairie Dog** is important to the ecosystem. Its digging allows air to circulate and promotes soil formation. It clips back brush to help keep prairie grass short. It is a keystone species, which means other animals in its ecosystem depend on it for survival, and it provides food and shelter for as many as 170 different animals. The Black-tailed Prairie Dog is the only species of prairie dog found in Texas, and it lives in deep burrows with funnel-shaped entrances and detailed tunnels. The main burrow entrances are marked by mounds with dirt walls around them. These mounds are often 12 in. (30 cm) high and help to keep flash floods from destroying the burrows. They also serve as lookout points.

Help the prairie dog find its burrow.

Word Search

The many different habitats of Texas, along with all the species that come there from the eastern and western United States and Mexico, make it one of the best places to find and study reptiles and amphibians. In total, there are over 225 species, including turtles, lizards, snakes, crocodilians, salamanders, frogs and toads.

Find the names of these reptiles and amphibians in the puzzle.

```
R S N D I N T S U K T U E T R R
O R R S B S L H O N D R F O R A
D O R O K L N I T S N A K E H O
I B A K Z A G L N G L R R H O L
G G H F O S A I O I E S G L G T
N U L R I L E A U T R O A K N I
E R D G D B R T R L D U N D O O
K G R L H R T U E A B R R L S N
L O O A G T E R O U K E N L E D
R K N I K S K T L I Z A R D L D
S Z D U S S N L K F I R O N E O
T R S N B T F E T O S O T N L I
E S I O T R O T T I D O N T N L
O U K N O D K R E O G S E A E O
E L O G E T E E S E K G I D L R
B A G E S O O G L A T Z T R D O
```

HOGNOSE

TURTLE

TOAD

SNAKE

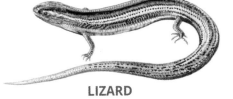

LIZARD

Answers

```
B A G E S O O G L A T Z T R D O
E L O G E T E E S E K G I D L R
O U K N O D K R E O G S E A E O
T N T N O D I T T O R T O I S E
L N T O S O T E F T B N S R T
O E N O R I F K L N S S U D Z S
D L D R A Z I L T K S K I N K R
N S L R R B A E U T R H L R G K
O O D N U D L R T R B D G D R E
I K N A K O R T U A E L I R L U N
T G L G S E I O I A S O F H G G
L O H R R L G N L G A Z K A B I
O H E K A N S T I L N L K O R O D
A R O F R D N O H L S B S R R O
R R T E U T K U S T N I D N S R
```

TORTOISE

SKINK

BULLFROG

Connect the Dots

Amphibians are smooth-skinned, limbed vertebrates that live in moist habitats and breathe through lungs, skin, gills or a combination of all three. While many spend much of their lives on land, they still depend on a watery environment to complete their life cycle. Most reproduce by laying eggs in or near water. The young hatch as swimming larvae that breathe through gills. After a short developmental period, the larvae metamorphose into young adults with lungs and legs.

I am a warty amphibian. My name rhymes with "load."
Follow the numbers to connect the dots and draw the mystery amphibian.

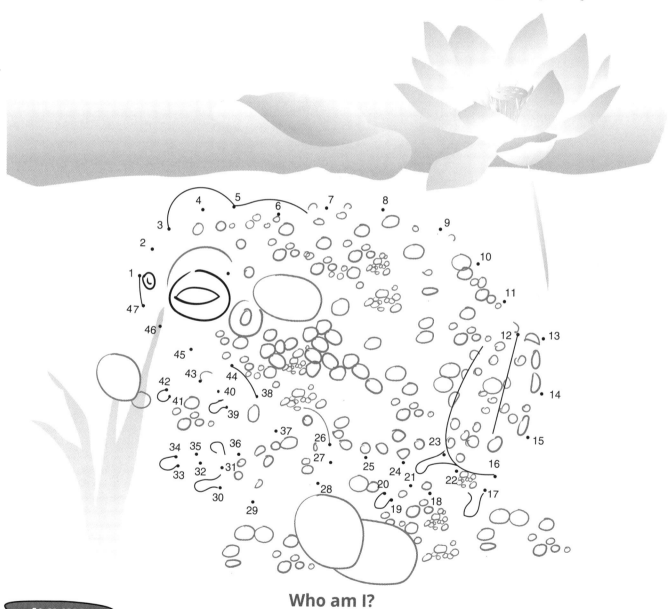

Who am I?

Answers

Be an Artist

Draw this Texas Horned Lizard by copying one square at a time.

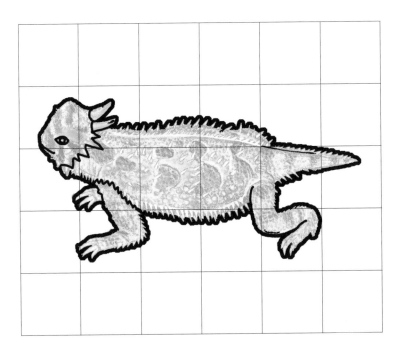

Lizards are scaly-skinned animals that usually have 4 legs and a tail, movable eyelids, visible ear openings, claws and toothed jaws. A few species are legless and resemble snakes. Texas's State Reptile, and the state's most well-known, is the **Texas Horned Lizard**. This lizard has spines down both sides of its body and two on its head that resemble horns. It lives in the sandy areas of the grasslands.

Crossword

Snakes play a very important role in the ecosystem. They are typically in the middle of the food web, being both predator and prey. Their predators are birds of prey, coyotes, raccoons, opossums as well as feral cats and hogs. As predators, and depending on their size and environment, snakes eat rodents, worms, insects, crayfish, fish, frogs, bird eggs and nestlings.

Use the clues about snakes to solve the puzzle.

Across

2. It is a small docile snake that is common in South Texas.
4. Its tail looks like a braided whip.
6. Immune to rattlesnake venom, it commonly feeds on rattlesnake.
7. It is also known as a spreading adder and is mildly venomous (poisonous).
8. It feeds on rodents and is valued for controlling the spread of mice by eating them.

Down

1. It is also often called a Black Snake.
3. It is a venomous pit viper species native to the Western United States.
5. To help recognize this venomous snake, people use this rhyme: "Red on yellow can kill a fellow."

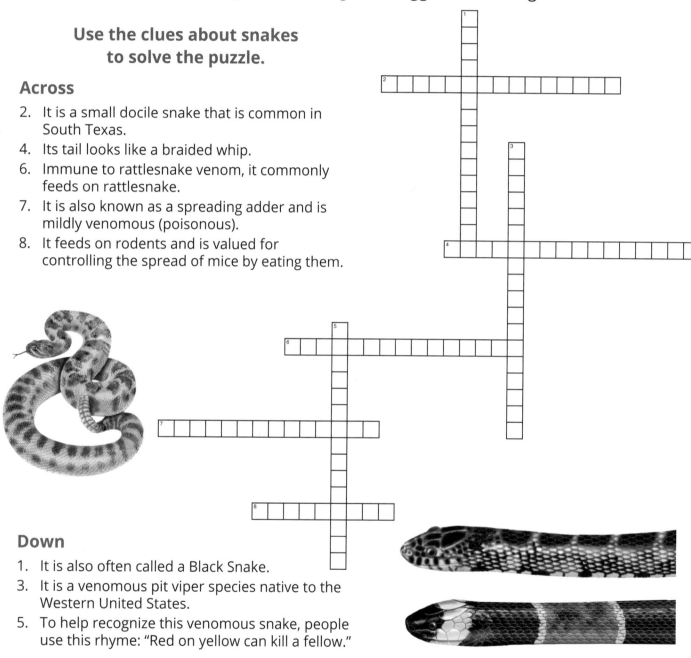

Who Am I?

Insects represent 60% of all life on earth and are a very important part of the animal kingdom. Many insects in the grasslands of Texas feed solely on the nectar of native plants. This is because they have lived here, alongside those plants, for thousands of years.

Draw a line between the grassland insect and its name.

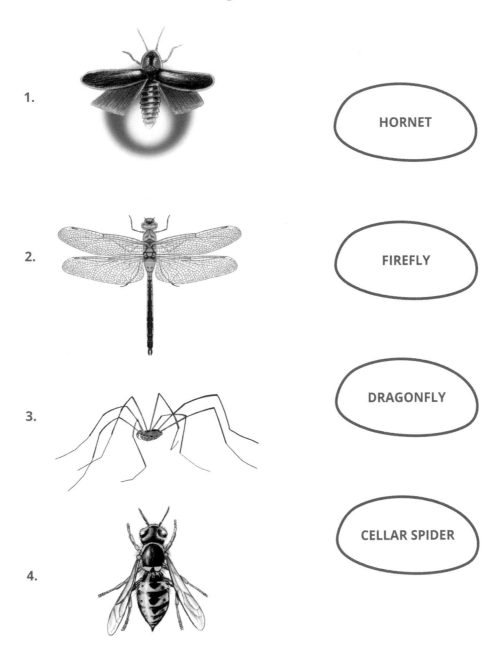

1.

2.

3.

4.

HORNET

FIREFLY

DRAGONFLY

CELLAR SPIDER

Word Search

Insects are invertebrates, which means they have no backbone or internal skeleton. Very adaptable creatures, they can survive extreme elements, including very hot or dry habitats. Many have adaptations (special body parts) that allow them to fly.

Find these grassland insects in the puzzle.

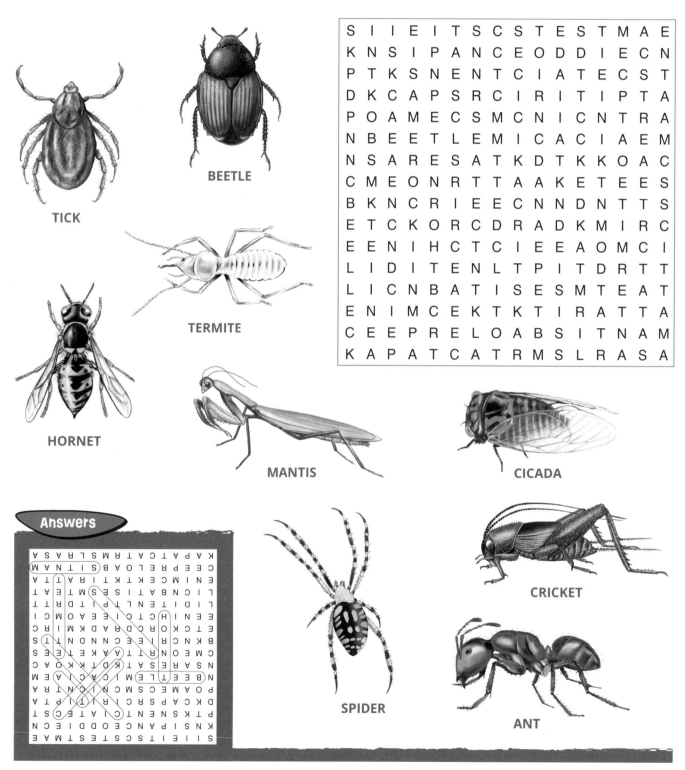

BEETLE

TICK

TERMITE

HORNET

MANTIS

CICADA

```
S I I E I T S C S T E S T M A E
K N S I P A N C E O D D I E C N
P T K S N E N T C I A T E C S T
D K C A P S R C I R I T I P T A
P O A M E C S M C N I C N T R A
N B E E T L E M I C A C I A E M
N S A R E S A T K D T K K O A C
C M E O N R T T A A K E T E E S
B K N C R I E E C N N D N T T S
E T C K O R C D R A D K M I R C
E E N I H C T C I E E A O M C I
L I D I T E N L T P I T D R T T
L I C N B A T I S E S M T E A T
E N I M C E K T K T I R A T T A
C E E P R E L O A B S I T N A M
K A P A T C A T R M S L R A S A
```

Answers

SPIDER

CRICKET

ANT

26

Connect the Dots

Texas has recorded more butterfly species than any other state, partly because of the many different kinds of habitats. Some species of butterfly rely on the open and sunny grassland habitat for their survival. The largest butterfly in Texas is the **Giant Swallowtail**.

Draw this prairie butterfly as it feeds on pollen and nectar from grassland wildflowers.

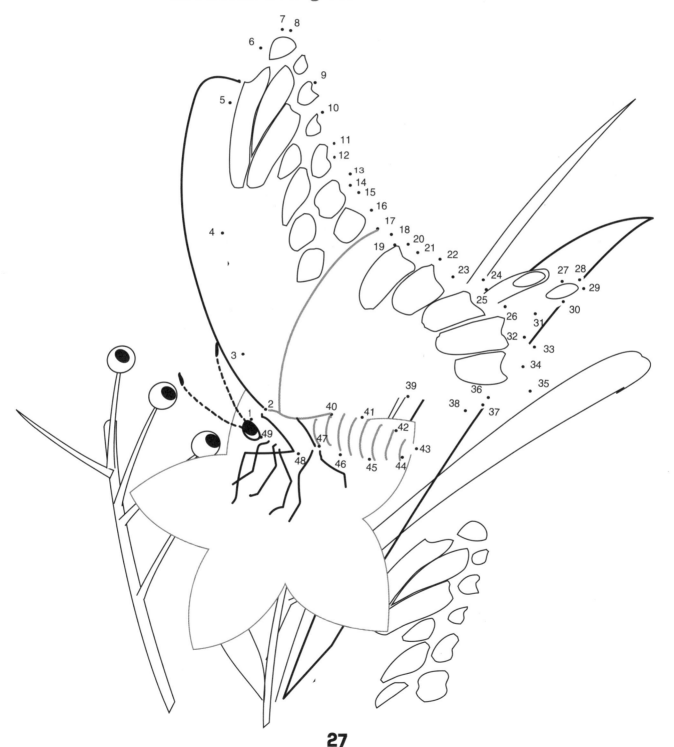

Butterflies and Moths

The two groups differ in several ways:

Butterflies	Moths
• Active by day	• Active at night
• Brightly colored	• Most are dull colored
• Thin body	• Stout body
• Rests with wings held erect over its back	• Rests with wings folded, tent-like, over its back
• Antennae are thin and thickened at the tip	• Antennae are usually thicker and often feathery

All butterflies and moths have a complex life cycle consisting of four developmental stages.

1. Eggs
2. Caterpillars (larvae)
3. Pupae (chrysalis/ cocoon)
4. Adult

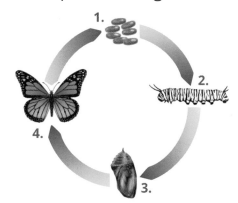

Attracting Butterflies to Your Yard

Food – Almost all butterfly caterpillars eat plants; adult butterflies feed almost only on plant nectar. Your library or local garden shop will have information on which plants attract which species.

Water – Soak the soil in your garden or sandy areas to create puddles. These provide a source of water and minerals.

Rocks – Put large flat rocks in sunny areas. Butterflies will gather there to spread their wings and warm up.

Brush – Small brush piles and hollow logs provide ideal places for butterflies to lay their eggs and hibernate over the winter.

Word Search

Find the names of these grassland butterflies and moths in the puzzle.

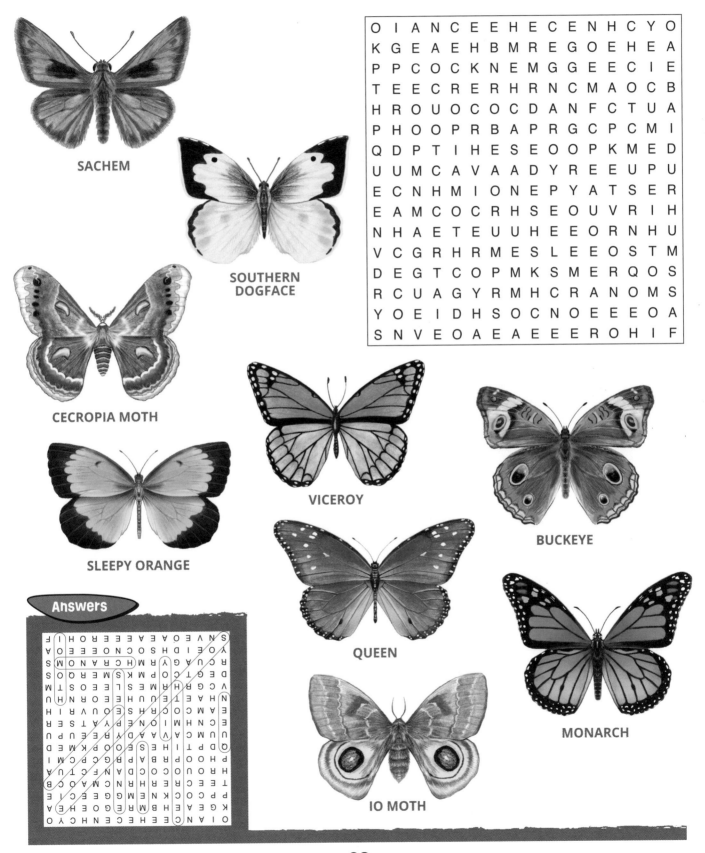

SACHEM

SOUTHERN DOGFACE

```
O I A N C E E H E C E N H C Y O
K G E A E H B M R E G O E H E A
P P C O C K N E M G G E E C I E
T E E C R E R H R N C M A O C B
H R O U O C O C D A N F C T U A
P H O O P R B A P R G C P C M I
Q D P T I H E S E O O P K M E D
U U M C A V A A D Y R E E U P U
E C N H M I O N E P Y A T S E R
E A M C O C R H S E O U V R I H
N H A E T E U U H E E O R N H U
V C G R H R M E S L E E O S T M
D E G T C O P M K S M E R Q O S
R C U A G Y R M H C R A N O M S
Y O E I D H S O C N O E E E O A
S N V E O A E A E E E R O H I F
```

CECROPIA MOTH

SLEEPY ORANGE

VICEROY

QUEEN

BUCKEYE

MONARCH

IO MOTH

Be an Artist

North America has 327 dragonfly species, and 160 of them can be found in Texas. Dragonflies and their smaller relatives, the damselflies, belong to the order Odonata, which comes from the Greek word for tooth. The **Giant Darner** is the largest dragonfly found in Texas, with a wingspan of more than five inches. There are fossils of dragonflies that lived 300 million years ago whose wingspan stretched more than two feet.

Draw this dragonfly by copying one square at a time.

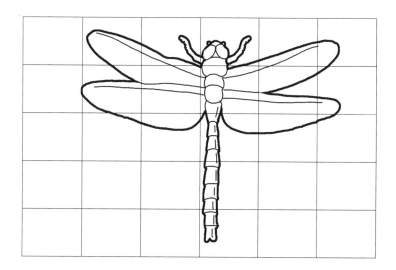

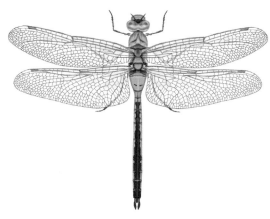

Color Me

The **Yellow Jacket** is an aggressive wasp that is very protective of its home. Taking its name from its bright coloring, it has a hairless body banded with yellow and black. The Texas Yellow Jacket builds its nest in the ground or in an enclosed hollow and will usually not chase or sting unless its nest is threatened.

Use the Color Key to help you color the picture of the Yellow Jacket.

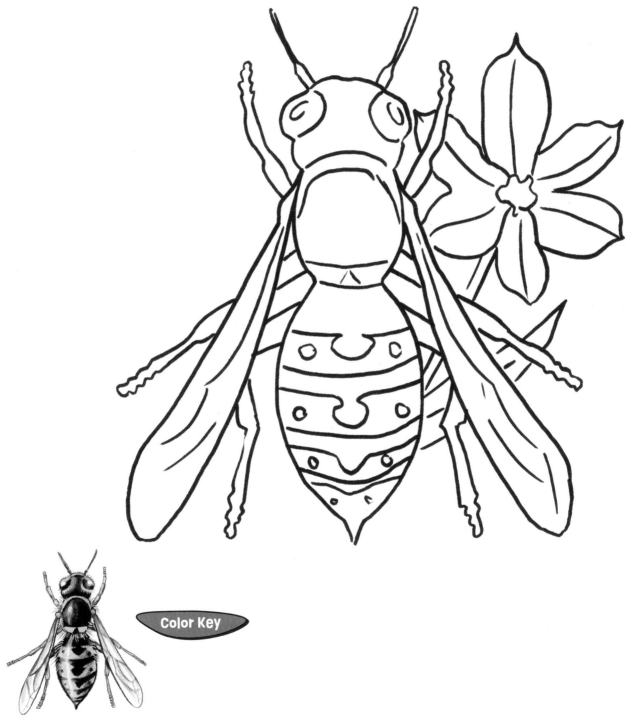

Color Key

Wildlife Respect

In wild spaces, humans are the visitors. We are lucky to be able to observe animals in their natural habitats. Along with that privilege, comes a responsibility to respect the animals we see, as well as their homes. The best way to learn about wildlife is by quietly watching. Though the possibility of getting a better look—or a better photo—can be tempting, getting too close can be stressful to a wild animal.

Here are some ways you can help reduce the number of disruptive human encounters that wild animals experience:

1. Know the site before you go.
2. When taking photos, do not use a flash, which can disturb animals.
3. Give animals room to move and act naturally.
4. Visit after breakfast and before dinner when wild animals are less active.
5. Do not touch or disturb the animals.
6. Do not feed the animals.
7. Store your food and take your trash with you.
8. Read and respect signs.
9. Do not make quick movements or loud noises.
10. Report any encounters with dangerous animals.